BEHIND THE PLATE

NATIONAL LEAGUE WEST

THE ARIZONA DIAMONDBACKS, THE COLORADO ROCKIES, THE LOS ANGELES DODGERS, THE SAN DIEGO PADRES, AND THE SAN FRANCISCO GIANTS

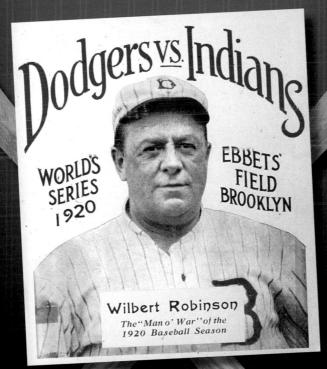

Dodgers vs. Indians

WORLD'S SERIES 1920

EBBETS FIELD BROOKLYN

Wilbert Robinson

The "Man o' War" of the 1920 Baseball Season

BY JIM GIGLIOTTI

Direct/Bcap Read 27.07 3/06

The Child's World

National League West: The Arizona Diamondbacks, the Colorado Rockies, the Los Angeles Dodgers, the San Diego Padres, and the San Francisco Giants
Published in the United States of America by The Child's World®
PO Box 326 • Chanhassen, MN 55317-0326 • 800-599-READ • www.childsworld.com

Acknowledgements:
The Child's World®: Mary Berendes, Publishing Director

Editorial Directions, Inc.: E. Russell Primm, Editorial Director; Matthew Messbarger, Line Editor; Katie Marsico, Assistant Editor; Susan Hindman, Copy Editor; Sarah E. De Capua, Proofreader; Kevin Cunningham, Fact Checker; Tim Griffin/IndexServ, Indexer; James Buckley Jr., Photo Researcher and Selector

The Design Lab: Kathleen Petelinsek, Art Direction and Design; Kari Thornborough, Page Production

Cover:
Barry Bonds

Page one:
Wilbert
Robinson

Photos:
AP: 36
Al Behrman/AP: 14
Bettmann/Corbis: 20, 23, 28, 29, 35, 37
Colin Braley/Reuters/Corbis: 9, 10
Chris Carlson/AP: 4
Tony Dejak/AP: 16
Richard Drew/AP: 26
Tom Hauck/Allsport/Getty: 38
Lenny Ignelzi/AP: 33
Jed Jacobsohn/Getty: 40
Rusty Kennedy/AP: 24
JT Lovette/Reuters/Corbis: 30
MLB/Getty: 27
National Baseball Hall of Fame/AP: 19, 34
Chris Pizzello/AP: 25
Gene J. Puskar/AP: 17
Transcendental Graphics: 1
Chris Trotman/NewSport/Corbis: 7
Kimberly White/Reuters/Corbis: Cover
David Zalubowski/AP: 13, 18

Library of Congress Cataloging-in-Publication Data
Gigliotti, Jim.
  National League West / by Jim Gigliotti.
    p. cm. — (Behind the plate)
  Includes index.
  ISBN 1-59296-363-3 (library bound : alk. paper) 1. National League of Professional Baseball Clubs—Juvenile literature. 2. Baseball teams—West (U.S.)—Juvenile literature. I. Title. II. Series.
  GV875.A3G55 2004
  796.357'092—dc22   2004016848

Table of Contents

Team: Arizona
Diamondbacks

Founded: 1998

Park: Bank One
Ballpark

Park Opened: 1998

Colors: Purple, teal,
and black

Team: Colorado
Rockies

Founded: 1993

Park: Coors Field

Park Opened: 1995

Colors: Black, silver,
and purple

At first glance, the West Division of Major League
Baseball's National League (NL) may appear to be
an unusual collection of very different franchises.
The Los Angeles Dodgers and the San Francisco
Giants, with their long and rich histories, are grouped
with relative newcomers, the Arizona Diamondbacks,
the Colorado Rockies, and the San Diego Padres. The
Dodgers, who are known for being pitching rich, are
mixed with the power-hitting Giants and Rockies. The
high-profile pitchers in Arizona go up against the youngsters in San Diego. Those differences, however, annually
make the NL West one
of baseball's most excit-
ing and competitive
divisions.

Until the Dodgers
and Giants moved
from New York in
1958, there was no
major league base-
ball on the West
Coast. There
was minor league
professional baseball
played at a high

Eric Gagne

level. Joe DiMaggio, for instance, was a star for the Pacific Coast League's San Francisco Seals before joining the New York Yankees. As far as the big leagues were concerned, though, the westernmost team was the St. Louis Cardinals.

The NL West originally was formed as a six-team division in 1969, when the league expanded from 10 to 12 teams with the addition of the Padres and the Montreal Expos. But West was West in name only. Oddly, the Atlanta Braves, Cincinnati Reds, and Houston Astros joined the Dodgers, Padres, and Giants.

Those teams made up the West until the 1993 season, when the Colorado Rockies, an **expansion team**, joined the group. The 104–win Braves edged the 103–win Giants in a thrilling division chase that year. Then Atlanta headed to the East when the NL realigned into three divisions (including the Central) in 1994. The NL West became a four-team group, consisting of Colorado, Los Angeles, San Diego, and San Francisco. Four years later, the expansion Diamondbacks made it a five-team group, and the division has remained that way ever since.

That's a quick overview of the division as a whole. Want to know more about the individual clubs? Read on, and you'll soon qualify as an expert on all the teams in the NL West.

CHAPTER ONE

The Arizona Diamondbacks

The expansion Arizona Diamondbacks debuted under Manager Buck Showalter in 1998. The NL West's newest addition had its good moments in that first season. For instance, they had a seven-game winning streak in late August and early September, which tied the longest ever by an expansion team. But Arizona won only 65 games that season and, as you might expect from a first-year club, finished last in the division, 33 games behind the champion Padres.

Other than their final record, though, there was little typical about the Diamondbacks in their early days. Unlike most expansion teams, they had an everyday lineup sprinkled with capable **veterans** such as third baseman Matt Williams, shortstop Jay Bell, and outfielder Devon White. They also had experienced pitchers such as Andy Benes, Omar Daal, and **closer** Gregg Olson.

Randy Johnson's arrival in 1999 made the Diamondbacks instant contenders.

Then, after the first season, came an important moment in the franchise's history when dominating left-handed starting pitcher Randy Johnson signed to play for the Diamondbacks. Johnson, a former American League (AL) **Cy Young Award** winner for Seattle, was one of the most coveted **free agents** available in the off-season. He had played out his contract in Houston following a midseason trade in 1998.

There's a picnic area just beyond the right-center field wall at Arizona's Bank One Ballpark . . . complete with a swimming pool!

Three in a row: Arizona's Jay Bell beat the Montreal Expos with a home run in the Diamondbacks' final at bat on May 10, 1999. The next night, Luis Gonzalez ended a game against the Expos with a home run. And the night after that, Matt Williams did the same thing.

Johnson's height (at 6 feet 10 inches, he's the tallest player in major league history) and his 100-mile-per-hour fastball make him a fearsome and intimidating presence on the mound. His arrival, plus those of outfielders Luis Gonzalez and Steve Finley, gave the Diamondbacks instant credibility.

That credibility quickly turned into victories on the field—and lots of them. Johnson won 17 games. (It would have been more if the Diamondbacks hadn't been shut out so many times in his starts.) He led the majors with 364 strikeouts on his way to the first of four straight NL Cy Young Awards. Gonzalez batted .336. Bell (38), Williams (35), and Finley (34) combined for 107 homers. Tony Womack led the league with 72 stolen bases. Arizona finished the season with a record of 100 wins and just 62 losses.

When the Diamondbacks beat the San Francisco Giants 11–3 on September 24, 1999, they clinched the NL West title. They became the first team ever to reach the **postseason** in just its second year. Though the club lost to the New York Mets in the first round of the playoffs, the groundwork for a championship had been laid.

The title came under new manager Bob Brenly two years later, after the arrival of the last piece

Steve Finley drove in a career-best 103 runs in his first season for Arizona in 1999.

This base hit by Arizona's Luis Gonzalez won the 2001 World Series.

Outfielder Luis
Gonzalez, who began
his big-league career
in 1990, never had hit
more than 31 home
runs in a season
until blasting a club-
record 57 in 2002.

of the championship puzzle: right-handed starting
pitcher Curt Schilling. Schilling actually had been
acquired midway through 2000, but Arizona missed
the playoffs that season. In 2001, however, he joined
Johnson to give the Diamondbacks one of the best
lefty–righty combos in baseball history. The pair
won 43 games while striking out 665 batters, and
Arizona edged the Giants to win the West.

After beating the Cardinals and Braves in the

NL playoffs, the Diamondbacks were in the World Series against the New York Yankees. Arizona won three times at home but lost three agonizing one-run games on the road to set up a deciding Game 7. In the bottom of the ninth, the Diamondbacks trailed the Yankees and their All-Star closer, Mariano Rivera, 2–1. After Arizona scored once to tie the game, Gonzalez lofted a single into shallow left-center field to drive in the winning run. He leapt for joy on the way to first base as Arizona won its first world title. Johnson and Schilling were both named Most Valuable Player (MVP) of the series.

The two were dominant again in 2002, when they combined to win 47 games and help the Diamondbacks win another division title. This time, though, they lost to the Cardinals in the opening round of the playoffs.

Arizona's best pitchers dropped off quite a bit in 2003, when both were injured. But young arms such as 24-year-old Brandon Webb stepped in. Schilling was then traded, and the Diamondbacks suffered through a poor season in 2004. Johnson, though, made history against Atlanta when he recorded the 17th perfect game ever—27 batters up and 27 batters down.

Curt Schilling beat Randy Johnson in a race to become the Diamondbacks' first 20-game winner. Schilling notched his 20th victory in a game against the Giants on September 5, 2001. Johnson won his 20th game later in the month.

Randy Johnson tied the major league record when he struck out 20 Cincinnati Reds in a game at Bank One Ballpark on May 8, 2001. He left after nine innings, though, with the score tied 3–3. Arizona won in 11 innings, 4–3.

CHAPTER TWO

The Colorado Rockies

The first time that a Colorado player ever stepped to the plate in a regular-season game, he hit a home run. That was Eric Young, and the Rockies haven't stopped swinging for the fences since.

No other team in baseball has had a more explosive hitting lineup than the Rockies since they entered the NL West as an expansion team in 1993. And no other team has had a more ineffective pitching staff.

In their first 11 seasons, the Rockies led the league in scoring five times, were second once, and never finished lower than fourth. But they also allowed the most runs nine times and never finished better than second-to-last in that category.

The reason lies primarily in the Rockies' home park. Coors Field in Denver rests 1 mile above sea level, and baseballs travel farther in the thin air. That means more home runs, and more home runs means higher scores. In fact, in 1999, the Rockies

Andres Galarraga, also known as the Big Cat, was a powerful offensive force for Colorado.

and their opponents combined to hit 303 home runs in 81 games at Coors Field. That was a single-season, big-league record, and it led to an average game score of 8–7 at the park.

Before Coors Field was completed, the Rockies played their first two seasons in Mile High Stadium—then the home of the National Football League's

Denver Broncos—with similar results. The only difference was at the gate, where the larger-capacity football stadium enabled a major league record crowd of 4,483,350 fans (an average of more than 55,000 per game) to watch the new team.

That team won a respectable 67 games under Manager Don Baylor. It was one of the best performances ever by a first-year expansion team and enabled the Rockies to escape the NL West **cellar.** They finished six games ahead of the San Diego Padres.

Former Montreal Expos and St. Louis Cardinals first baseman Andres Galarraga was the team's hitting star, batting a league-leading .370 with 98 runs batted in (RBIs). But the pitching staff allowed nearly six runs per game (5.97), or about one run per game worse than any other team in the league.

That would become a familiar refrain over the years, as the Rockies produced several great hitters to follow Galarraga. Outfielder Ellis Burks had a career year in 1996, when he led the league in runs, extra-base hits, and slugging percentage. Outfielder Larry Walker led the league in batting three times from

Larry Walker is best known for his big bat, but he shows here that he can play defense, too.

Opposing pitchers twice tossed no-hitters against the Rockies in 1996. But Colorado still finished with the league's highest batting average. That combination never happened before ... or since.

First baseman Andres Galarraga tied a big-league record when he homered in three consecutive innings in a game against the Padres on June 25, 1995.

It's not a surprise that the highest-scoring All-Star Game in history was played in Colorado. The AL All-Stars beat the NL All-Stars 13–8 at Coors Field in 1998.

1998 to 2001 and in homers in 1997, when he was the league MVP. First baseman Todd Helton led the NL in average, on-base percentage, slugging percentage, and RBIs in 2000.

Except for 1995, however, such a barrage of hitting has not translated into success in the win column. That year, the Rockies went 77–67 (the season started late after 1994's work stoppage) to earn a **wild-card** playoff berth. But they were eliminated in the NL

Todd Helton led the league by batting .372 with 147 RBIs in a remarkable 2000 season.

Young Jason Jennings gives the Rockies hope that their pitching staff is turning the corner.

Division Series by the Atlanta Braves—it was the lone postseason appearance in the Rockies' brief history.

Since 1997, they haven't finished higher than fourth place in the division. Their powerful offense continues to make opponents take notice, but they have not found enough consistent pitching. One recent bright spot, though, is young pitcher Jason Jennings. A first-round draft pick in 1999, Jennings was the NL's Rookie of the Year in 2002, when he went 16–8.

On September 12, 1996, Ellis Burks became the first 30–30 player (30 home runs and 30 stolen bases in the same season) in club history. The next day, fellow outfielder Dante Bichette became the second.

Preston Wilson had a breakout season after joining the Rockies in 2003.

In 2003, the Rockies won only 74 games
under current manager Clint Hurdle, but they
found another new hitting star in outfielder
Preston Wilson. After being acquired from the
Florida Marlins prior to the season, Wilson blasted
a career-best 36 home runs and led the NL by
driving in 141 runs in his first year in Colorado.

CHAPTER THREE

The Los Angeles Dodgers

From Brooklyn to Los Angeles, the Dodgers franchise has had a big impact on major league history. On the field, the Dodgers have won six world championships and made 23 playoff appearances. Off the field, they have helped shape the sport culturally, from its **integration** in 1947 to its move to the West Coast in 1958.

The Brooklyn Dodgers still are remembered fondly by longtime residents of the New York City area. Players such as outfielder Zach Wheat, first baseman Dolph Camilli, pitcher Preacher Roe, and outfielder Duke Snider—plus Ebbets Field, the Dodgers' home from 1913 to 1957—are recalled with considerable warmth.

Those Dodgers, however, played second fiddle to the AL's mighty New York Yankees most of the time. Though Brooklyn

EDWIN DONALD SNIDER
"DUKE"
BROOKLYN N.L., LOS ANGELES N.L.,
NEW YORK N.L., SAN FRANCISCO N.L.,
1947-1964
HIT 407 CAREER HOME RUNS AND TIED N.L.
RECORD WITH 40 OR MORE ROUND-TRIPPERS
FIVE YEARS IN A ROW, 1953-1957. BATTED .300
OR BETTER SEVEN TIMES IN COMPILING .295
LIFETIME AVERAGE. TOPPED LEAGUE IN SLUGG-
ING PCT. TWICE AND TOTAL BASES THREE TIMES.
FIRST TO HIT FOUR HOMERS IN A WORLD SERIES
TWICE --IN 1952 AND 1955. SET N.L.
RECORD FOR SERIES HOMERS (11).

Jackie Robinson joined the Dodgers' Montreal farm club in 1946; one year later, he made history when he integrated the major leagues.

Dodgers shortstop Maury Wills set a big-league record (since broken) when he stole 104 bases in 1962.

won five NL **pennants** between 1941 and 1953, they lost to the Yankees in the World Series each time. "Wait 'Till Next Year" became the club's unofficial rallying cry.

"Next year" finally arrived in 1955, when Johnny Podres pitched a complete-game shutout against the

Yankees in Game 7. Defensive replacement Sandy Amoros made a spectacular catch and throw to preserve the Dodgers' 2–0 victory. Things returned to form the next year, though, when the Yankees avenged that defeat. Two seasons later, the Dodgers were in Los Angeles.

The move to the West Coast in 1958 wasn't the first time that the Dodgers had a huge effect on the baseball world. Only 11 seasons earlier, in 1947, the Dodgers and Jackie Robinson shattered baseball's color barrier. Until then, African Americans had been prevented from playing in the majors, by agreement among team owners. Two years after that, Robinson joined teammates Don Newcombe (a pitcher) and Roy Campanella (a catcher) as the first African Americans to represent the NL in the All-Star Game.

Since moving to L.A., the Dodgers have had a consistent grip on their fans, often drawing more than 3 million customers in a season. The club played in the enormous Los Angeles Memorial Coliseum its first two years on the West Coast. They won a World Series against the Chicago White Sox that drew record crowds of more than 90,000 in 1959. They then moved into Dodger Stadium in 1962. Since then,

The Dodgers were known by various names, including the "Bridegrooms" and the "Superbas." They permanently took on their current nickname in 1932, so called for the way Brooklynites had to dodge trolley cars in the street.

Sandy Koufax tossed four no-hitters in his career. Only Nolan Ryan (with seven) pitched more.

Chicago's Rick Monday prevented two men from burning an American flag in the outfield at Dodger Stadium in 1976. Monday later played eight seasons for Los Angeles.

In 1977, Dodgers outfielders Dusty Baker and Glenn Burke helped launch a cultural phenomenon. After Baker's homer, he and Burke slapped palms high above their heads at home plate. Soon, athletes everywhere were doing the "high five."

Los Angeles has produced lots of star pitchers who have made the club what it is today.

Sandy Koufax and Don Drysdale were the big names in the 1960s, as were Don Sutton and Burt Hooton in the 1970s. Then came Fernando Valenzuela and Orel Hershiser in the 1980s, and Hideo Nomo and Kevin Brown in the 1990s.

In the early 1980s, Mexican native Valenzuela broke into the big leagues while still a teenager, and "Fernandomania" helped draw thousands of Hispanic fans to Dodger Stadium. A decade after that, Nomo became the first Japan League star to make the majors, and "Nomomania" gripped southern California.

But Koufax was the biggest star of all of them. He won 111 games from 1962 to 1966 and earned three Cy Young Awards. He was just 30 years old and at the height of his career when arthritis in his pitching arm forced him to stop playing. He retired following a 1966 season in which he won 27 games with an earned run average (ERA) of 1.73. In 1972, he became the youngest player ever elected to the Hall of Fame.

Koufax and Drysdale helped Manager Walter Alston's Dodgers win the World Series in 1959,

Sandy Koufax was a dominant pitcher until injuries sped up his retirement at age 30.

Kirk Gibson's World Series homer in 1988 is one of baseball's most memorable moments.

From 1992 to 1996, five consecutive Dodgers—Eric Karros, Mike Piazza, Raul Mondesi, Hideo Nomo, and Todd Hollandsworth—earned NL Rookie of the Year honors.

Orel Hershiser closed the 1988 season with a major league record of 59 consecutive scoreless innings. The previous mark of 58.2 innings was held by former Dodgers pitcher Don Drysdale.

1963, and 1965. The club also won the Fall Classic (another name, though unofficial, for the World Series) under Tommy Lasorda in 1981 and 1988. In the latter year, the Dodgers were the heavy **underdog** team to the Oakland A's, but Hershiser's gritty pitching led the way. In Game 1, injured and limping pinch-hitter Kirk Gibson's dramatic, game-winning home run in the bottom of the ninth inning sparked Los Angeles to victory.

The ensuing years have not been as kind to the Dodgers. Since beating Oakland in Game 5 to clinch the 1988 World Series, they have not won another postseason series. And they entered 2004 without a playoff appearance since 1997. They traded away stars such as Pedro Martinez, who went on to win three Cy Young Awards for the Expos and Red Sox, and Mike Piazza, perhaps the greatest hitting catcher in baseball history.

Odalis Perez has emerged as one of baseball's best left-handed pitchers.

Outfielder Shawn Green is a favorite among Dodgers fans.

Dodgers closer Eric
Gagne converted a
major league record
84 consecutive save
opportunities from
2002 to 2004.

But the current Dodgers have another big pitching star in closer Eric Gagne, the NL Cy Young Award winner was the league's best pitcher in 2003. That year, he successfully converted all 55 of his **save** chances. And with third baseman Adrian Beltre (who had a breakout year with 48 home runs) and outfielder Shawn Green providing capable hitting, Los Angeles edged San Francisco to win the 2004 NL West crown.

CHAPTER FOUR

The San Diego Padres

Winning came relatively quickly for the 1990s NL West expansion franchises in Arizona and Colorado. However, the expansion San Diego Padres of 1969 did not meet with such immediate success. In fact, it took a long time for the Padres to reward their patient fans with a playoff season. When they did, though, it made it all the more sweet.

San Diego debuted with a record of 52 wins and 110 losses under Manager Preston Gomez in 1969. The Padres were in the NL West cellar that year—the next-closest team was a full 29 games in front of them. Though San Diego had a couple of stars in young first baseman Nate Colbert and outfielder Ollie Brown, things didn't get much better in the ensuing seasons.

Five more consecutive last-place finishes followed under Gomez, Don

Rollie Fingers

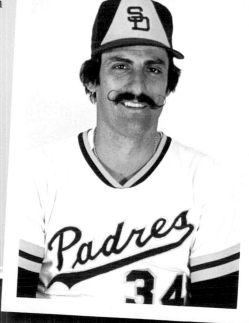

**Relief pitcher Goose Gossage helped the Padres
win the NL pennant for the first time in 1984.**

Zimmer, and John McNamara. Worse than
that was the fan apathy that contributed to
declining attendance and, eventually, the sale of
the team in 1974 to a buyer who planned to move
the club to Washington, D.C.

McDonald's owner Ray Kroc stepped in, though,
to purchase the franchise and keep it in San Diego.
Things began improving, both at the gate and on
the field. In 1978, the club was bolstered by the

emergence of slugging outfielder Dave Winfield and slick-fielding infielder Ozzie Smith. Closer Rollie Fingers anchored the bullpen. All three players were future Hall of Famers. With them on board, Manager Roger Craig's Padres won more games (84) than they lost (78) for the first time.

San Diego failed to build on that success, however, and it wasn't until 1984 that the Padres reached the playoffs. A new cast of players—including outfielder

After playing parts of 14 seasons in Los Angeles,
Steve Garvey joined San Diego in 1983.

Tony Gwynn, first baseman Steve Garvey, **ace** starting pitcher Eric Show, and closer Goose Gossage—had been assembled under Manager Dick Williams. The Padres went 92–70 to coast to their first division title, winning by 12 games.

That year, Gwynn batted .351 to win the first of his eight career batting titles, Show won a team-leading 15 games, and Gossage saved 25 games. At 35, Garvey, the former Los Angeles Dodgers star, hit only eight regular-season home runs. But he belted a memorable round-tripper to win Game 4 of the NL playoffs, which tied the NL Championship Series against Chicago. The next day, the Padres denied the ill-fated Cubs what would have been their first World Series appearance since 1945. San Diego reached the Fall Classic for the first time by rallying from a 3–0 deficit to win Game 5, 6–3.

However, the Detroit Tigers routed the Padres in five games in the World Series. San Diego did not return to the postseason until 1996, when they won the division in dramatic fashion under Manager Bruce Bochy. Assured of at least a wild-card berth, but trailing the division-leading Dodgers by two

Tony Gwynn was a hitting machine for the Padres, batting .338 in his 20-year career.

In 1976, San Diego veteran Randy Jones won the Cy Young Award as the NL's best pitcher. His teammate, Butch Metzger, was the league's Rookie Pitcher of the Year.

The San Diego Chicken was the mascot who spawned similar entertainers in ballparks all across the country. Ted Giannoulas began performing antics in the costume for crowds at Qualcomm Stadium (then known as San Diego Jack Murphy Stadium) in 1974.

games, with three to play, San Diego swept three games in Los Angeles to win the West. St. Louis ended the Padres' pennant hopes, though, with a sweep in the first round of the playoffs. The Padres' next World Series appearance came in 1998, when they were swept in four games by the New York Yankees.

Gwynn, a soft-spoken star and a leader in the community, bridged the gap between the Padres' pennant-winning teams. He could have made more money playing elsewhere, but he chose to remain in San Diego for his entire 20-year career, from 1982 to 2001. He's now the head coach at his alma mater, San Diego State University.

The likeable outfielder was perhaps the finest pure hitter of his time. He batted .338 in his 20-year career, never falling below .300 after hitting .289 in 190 at bats as a rookie and topped by a .394 mark in 1994, the majors' best in 53 years. An excellent all-around athlete who also played basketball in college, Gwynn possessed deceptive speed (he once stole 56 bases in a season) and an accurate arm. In NL history, only the legendary Honus Wagner can match Gwynn's eight batting titles. He is a certain first-ballot Hall of Famer when he becomes eligible in 2007.

Young third baseman Sean Burroughs is one of San Diego's brightest stars.

The Padres haven't made the playoffs since winning the 1998 pennant. But hopes were high as the club moved into new Petco Park in 2004. San Diego has lots of good, young pitching arms, up-and-coming hitters such as third baseman Sean Burroughs, and a core center of veterans led by slugging outfielder Brian Giles, a late-season acquisition in 2003.

In 1991, Padres first baseman Fred McGriff became only the fourth player in big-league history to hit grand slams (home runs with the bases loaded) in back-to-back games.

CHAPTER FIVE

The San Francisco Giants

The history of the Giants franchise is a tale of two cities, New York and San Francisco. And since moving to the West Coast in 1958, that tale has included the best of times and the worst of times.

The Giants enjoyed great success when the club was in New York and not so much since moving to San Francisco. From 1972 to 1986, the Giants suffered through the most prolonged period with no success in their franchise history. They posted only four winning seasons in that span and never finished higher than third place. In recent years, though, the Giants' fortunes have taken a tremendous surge upward again.

In fact, since a last-place finish in 1996, the Giants have been among baseball's most consistent winners. Under

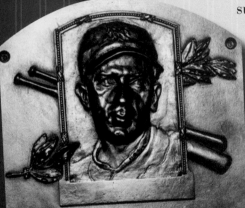

CARL HUBBELL
NEW YORK N.L. 1928-1943
HAILED FOR IMPRESSIVE PERFORMANCE IN
1934 ALL-STAR GAME WHEN HE STRUCK OUT
RUTH, GEHRIG, FOXX, SIMMONS AND CRONIN
IN SUCCESSION. NICKNAMED GIANTS'
MEAL-TICKET. WON 253 GAMES IN MAJORS
SCORING 16 STRAIGHT IN 1936. COMPILED
STREAK OF 46⅓ SCORELESS INNINGS IN
1933. HOLDER OF MANY RECORDS.

Under the watchful eye of Manager John McGraw, the Giants
won 10 pennants between 1904 and 1924.

Manager Dusty Baker, they reached the postseason three times from 1997 to 2002, highlighted
by the NL pennant in 2002. Then, in 2003, new
manager Felipe Alou, a star outfielder for the club
in the 1960s, led the team to 100 wins and the
West Division title.

The Giants have become big winners at the
box office, too. After many years of playing in cold,

The franchise's
original nickname
was the Gothams. But
Manager Jim Mutrie
dubbed his team
"my Giants" during
a close pennant race
in 1885, and the
nickname stuck.

Mel Ott slugged 511 homers in his 22-year career (1926–1947) for the Giants.

windy Candlestick Park, the club moved into new
Pac Bell Park (now called SBC Park) in 2000. The
Giants won the West in the first year in their new
home and have drawn more than 3 million fans each
season there.

The roots of the Giants franchise go back to 1883.
By early in the 20th century, the New York club was

one of baseball's most successful franchises. The
Giants finished first or second in the NL 20 times
under legendary manager John McGraw between
1903 and 1931, and won the World Series three times.
McGraw's players included future Hall of Fame stars

A gentle giant off the field, Willie McCovey was a fearsome sight
to opposing pitchers while at the plate.

Legendary outfielder Willie Mays has his own statue outside San Francisco's SBC Park.

such as pitchers Christy Mathewson and Carl Hubbell and sluggers Mel Ott and Bill Terry.

Terry took over as manager early in the 1932 season and led the Giants to another World Series title the next year. In 1954, the Giants won their fifth world championship—third at the time behind only the New York Yankees and St. Louis Cardinals. Four years later, however, the Giants moved to San Francisco, and they haven't won the World Series since.

It's not as if they haven't come close, though. In 1962, they won the NL pennant and then took the Yankees to seven games in the World Series. In the bottom of the ninth inning of the final game, with the tying and winning runs in scoring position, New York second baseman Bobby Richardson snared Willie McCovey's line drive to end the game. From 1965 to 1969, the Giants finished in second place. In 1989, the Giants won their first pennant in 27 seasons. The Bay Bridge World Series was interrupted by a massive earthquake, and the Oakland A's eventually swept the Giants in four games. In 2002, San Francisco won another NL pennant and led Anaheim three games to two in the World Series. The Giants took a 5–0 lead into the seventh inning

Nearly 100 years after the fact, Christy Mathewson's performance for the New York Giants in the 1905 World Series remains one of the great pitching feats of all time. Mathewson tossed three shutouts in six days to lead the Giants past the Philadelphia Athletics.

In 1963, the Giants had the first all-brother outfield in big-league history: Jesus, Matty, and Felipe Alou.

Though the franchise has long been known for its powerful hitters, the 2004 Giants featured one of baseball's best pitchers in fireballer Jason Schmidt.

Willie Mays's over-the-shoulder catch in Game 1 of the 1954 World Series is perhaps the most memorable defensive play in baseball history. The grab sparked the Giants to a four-game sweep of Cleveland that year.

of Game 6, but the Angels rallied to win the game, then went on to take the series in Game 7.

No matter where they've been based, the one constant on Giants teams has been a list of sluggers destined for baseball's Hall of Fame. The Giants have produced some of the most successful home-run hitters—Mel Ott, Willie Mays, Willie McCovey, Orlando Cepeda, and Barry Bonds.

Of course, the most famous slugger in Giants history might be Bobby Thomson, though it's mostly for just one homer, dubbed the "Shot Heard 'Round the World." At the Polo Grounds in New York, Thomson's three-run home run came in the bottom of the ninth inning. It was the third and final game of a playoff against the Brooklyn Dodgers, and Thomson's homer gave the Giants the NL pennant on October 3, 1951.

Bonds's legacy eventually may surpass each of the club's other big home-run hitters, however. In 2001, he set baseball's single-season record by hitting an astounding 73 home runs. The next year, he won his first batting title by hitting .370, and he set another record for on-base percentage at .582.

Bonds turned 40 in 2004, but showed no signs of slowing down. He hit .362 to win his second batting title, belted 45 home runs, and broke his own record with an on-base percentage of .609. He also became only the third player to reach 700 home runs for his career, finishing the year at 703. The only players ever with more were Hank Aaron (755) and Babe Ruth (714).

San Francisco's Gaylord Perry tossed a no-hitter against St. Louis on September 17, 1968. The next day, the Cardinals' Ray Washburn no-hit the Giants!

Willie McCovey belted 18 career grand slams, the most in NL history.

Stat Stuff

TEAM RECORDS (THROUGH 2004)

Team	All-time Record	World Series Titles (Most Recent)	Number of Times in the Postseason	Top Manager (Wins)
Arizona	575–559	1 (2001)	3	Bob Brenly (303)
Colorado	882–999	0	1	Don Baylor (440)
Los Angeles*	9,635–8,727	6 (1988)	23	Walter Alston (2,040)
San Diego	2,611–3,094	0	3	Bruce Bochy (781)
San Francisco**	9,962–8,461	5 (1954)	23	John McGraw (2,583)

*includes Brooklyn
**includes New York

NATIONAL LEAGUE WEST
CAREER LEADERS (THROUGH 2004)

Arizona

Category	Name (Years with Team)	Total
Batting Average	Greg Colbrunn (1999–2002, 2004)	.310
Home Runs	Luis Gonzalez (1999–2004)	185
RBI	Luis Gonzalez (1999–2004)	622
Stolen Bases	Tony Womack (1999–2003)	182
Wins	Randy Johnson (1999–2004)	103
Saves	Matt Mantei (1999–2004)	74
Strikeouts	Randy Johnson (1999–2004)	1,832

NATIONAL LEAGUE WEST CAREER LEADERS (THROUGH 2004)

Colorado

Category	Name (Years with Team)	Total
Batting Average	Todd Helton (1997–2004)	.339
Home Runs	Larry Walker (1995–2004)	258
RBI	Larry Walker (1995–2004)	848
Stolen Bases	Eric Young (1993–1997)	180
Wins	Pedro Astacio (1997–2001)	53
Saves	Jose Jimenez (2000–03)	102
Strikeouts	Pedro Astacio (1997–2001)	749

Los Angeles

Category	Name (Years with Team)	Total
Batting Average	Willie Keeler (1893, 1899–1902)	.352
Home Runs	Duke Snider (1947–1962)	389
RBI	Duke Snider (1947–1962)	1,271
Stolen Bases	Maury Wills (1959–1966, 1969–1972)	490
Wins	Don Sutton (1966–1980, 1988)	233
Saves	Eric Gagne (1999–2004)	152
Strikeouts	Don Sutton (1966–1980, 1988)	2,696

STAT STUFF

NATIONAL LEAGUE WEST CAREER LEADERS (THROUGH 2004)

San Diego

Category	Name (Years with Team)	Total
Batting Average	Tony Gwynn (1982–2001)	.338
Home Runs	Nate Colbert (1969–1974)	163
RBI	Tony Gwynn (1982–2001)	1,138
Stolen Bases	Tony Gwynn (1982–2001)	319
Wins	Eric Show (1981–1990)	100
Saves	Trevor Hoffman (1993–2004)	350
Strikeouts	Andy Benes (1989–1995)	1,036

San Francisco

Category	Name (Years with Team)	Total
Batting Average	Bill Terry (1923–1936)	.341
Home Runs	Willie Mays (1951–1972)	646
RBI	Mel Ott (1926–1947)	1,860
Stolen Bases	Mike Tiernan (1887–1899)	428
Wins	Christy Mathewson (1900–1916)	372
Saves	Trevor Hoffman (1993–2004)	391
Strikeouts	Christy Mathewson (1900–1916)	2,499

Glossary

ace—the best pitcher on a baseball team

cellar—last place

closer—a relief pitcher brought in at the end of the game to save a victory

Cy Young Award—the award annually given to the best pitcher in each league

expansion team—a new franchise that starts from scratch, thus increasing (or expanding) the total number of clubs in a given league

free agents—players who have completed their contracts with one team and are free to sign with any other team

integration—opening something up to people of all races (in baseball's case, opening the game to African Americans in 1947) and ethnic groups

no-hitters—complete games in which the pitcher or pitchers for one team do not allow the opposing team any hits

pennants—the championships of each league (American and National)

postseason—the playoffs, which start with the Division Series, continue with the League Championship Series, and conclude with the World Series

professional—describes someone who receives pay for his or her services or activities; in this case, playing baseball as a livelihood

save—the action of a relief pitcher in successfully protecting a team's lead

underdog—a team that is not expected to win

veterans—players who have been in the game for many years

wild card—a team that finishes in second place in its division but still makes the playoffs

World Series—baseball's championship event; the winners of the AL and the NL pennants annually meet in a best-of-seven series to determine the world champion

Time Line

1883   The Giants franchise begins play in New York as the Gothams.

1884   The Dodgers franchise begins play in Brooklyn as the Atlantics.

1905   The Giants win the first of five World Series they won while in New York.

1951   The Giants' Bobby Thomson belts the "Shot Heard 'Round the World" to win the NL pennant.

1954   The Giants win their fifth—and, to date, last—World Series.

1955   After several near-misses, the Dodgers win the World Series for the first time.

1958   The Giants and Dodgers become the first big-league teams to move to the West Coast.

1959   The Dodgers win the first World Series of the five they won while in Los Angeles.

1969   The Padres join the NL as an expansion team, and the NL West is formed.

1988   Kirk Gibson's dramatic home run sparks the Dodgers to upset the Oakland A's in the World Series.

1993   The Colorado Rockies begin play as an expansion team.

1995   The Rockies reach the playoffs in just their third season, a record.

1998   The Arizona Diamondbacks begin play as an expansion team.

1999   The Diamondbacks reach the playoffs in only their second season, breaking the Rockies' record.

2001   The Diamondbacks win their first World Series by beating the New York Yankees in seven games.

For More Information

BOOKS

Delsohn, Steve. *True Blue: The Dramatic History of the Los Angeles Dodgers, Told by the Men Who Lived It.* New York: Morrow, 2001.

DeMarco, Tony. *Larry Walker.* Philadelphia: Chelsea House Publishers, 1999.

Goodman, Michael E. *The History of the San Diego Padres.* Mankato, Minn.: Creative Education, 1999.

Kelley, James. *Baseball.* New York: Dorling Kindersley Publishing, 2000.

Schott, Tom, and Nick Peters. *The Giants Encyclopedia.* Champaign, Ill.: Sports Publishing, 1999.

ON THE WEB

Visit our home page for lots of links about the National League West teams: *http://www.childsworld.com/links.html*

Note to Parents, Teachers, and Librarians: We routinely check our Web links to make sure they're safe, active sites—so encourage your readers to check them out!

Index

ABOUT THE AUTHOR

Jim Gigliotti is a former editor at the National Football League who now is a freelance writer based in southern California. Though he also has worked for the University of Southern California and the Los Angeles Dodgers, he is a lifelong San Francisco Giants fan. His recent writing credits include *Baseball: A Celebration* (with James Buckley Jr.) and several books for youngsters on NASCAR history and personalities.